BIRD VIEWING AREAS

Biodiversity in the Eastern coastal waters is exceptional. From the Grand Banks of Newfoundland where over 10,000,000 shorebirds can be found nesting in summer, to the pelagic birding opportunities offered by the warm waters of the Gulf Stream, to the mangrove forests and seagrass beds of the South Florida/Bahamian Atlantic Region where tropical species abound, the Eastern Coastal region is impressive and compelling for its unique and spectacular array of birds.

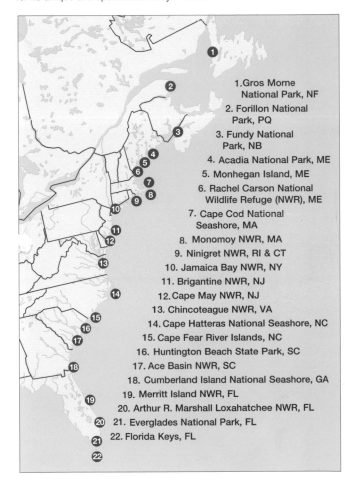

1. Gros Morne National Park, NF
2. Forillon National Park, PQ
3. Fundy National Park, NB
4. Acadia National Park, ME
5. Monhegan Island, ME
6. Rachel Carson National Wildlife Refuge (NWR), ME
7. Cape Cod National Seashore, MA
8. Monomoy NWR, MA
9. Ninigret NWR, RI & CT
10. Jamaica Bay NWR, NY
11. Brigantine NWR, NJ
12. Cape May NWR, NJ
13. Chincoteague NWR, VA
14. Cape Hatteras National Seashore, NC
15. Cape Fear River Islands, NC
16. Huntington Beach State Park, SC
17. Ace Basin NWR, SC
18. Cumberland Island National Seashore, GA
19. Merritt Island NWR, FL
20. Arthur R. Marshall Loxahatchee NWR, FL
21. Everglades National Park, FL
22. Florida Keys, FL

Waterford Press publishes reference guides that introduce readers to nature observation, outdoor recreation and survival skills. Product information is featured on the website: www.waterfordpress.com

Text & illustrations © 2022 Waterford Press. All rights reserved. Photos © Shutterstock. To order or for information on custom published products please call 800-434-2555 or email orderdesk@waterfordpress.com. For permissions or to share comments email info@waterfordpress.com.

978-1-62005-553-3 $7.95 U.S.

Kavanagh/Leung

EASTERN COASTAL BIRDS

A Waterproof Folding Guide to Familiar Species

WATERBIRDS

Winter / Summer

Common Loon
Gavia immer To 3 ft. (90 cm)

Red-throated Loon
Gavia stellata To 25 in. (63 cm)

Pied-billed Grebe
Podilymbus podiceps To 13 in. (33 cm)
Note banded white bill.

Red-necked Grebe
Podiceps grisegena To 19 in. (48 cm)

Mute Swan
Cygnus olor To 5 ft. (1.5 m)
Introduced resident species.

Horned Grebe
Podiceps auritus To 15 in. (38 cm)
Note reddish neck and ear tufts.

Tundra Swan
Cygnus columbianus To 4.5 ft. (1.4 m)
Note yellow mark on black bill.

Brant
Branta bernicla To 26 in. (65 cm)
Note white neck mark.

Northern Pintail
Anas acuta To 29 in. (73 cm)

Canada Goose
Branta canadensis To 45 in. (1.14 m)

Snow Goose
Chen caerulescens To 31 in. (78 cm)

Mallard
Anas platyrhynchos To 28 in. (70 cm)

WATERBIRDS

Green-winged Teal
Anas crecca To 16 in. (40 cm)

American Black Duck
Anas rubripes To 25 in. (63 cm)

Redhead
Aythya americana To 22 in. (55 cm)

Mottled Duck
Anas fulvigula To 20 in. (50 cm)
Brown duck has a yellow bill.

Wood Duck
Aix sponsa To 20 in. (50 cm)

Long-tailed Duck
Clangula hyemalis To 22 in. (55 cm)

Northern Shoveler
Spatula clypeata To 20 in. (50 cm)
Named for its large spatulate bill.

Canvasback
Aythya valisineria To 2 ft. (60 cm)
Note sloping forehead and black bill.

American Wigeon
Mareca americana To 23 in. (58 cm)

Ring-necked Duck
Aythya collaris To 18 in. (45 cm)
Note white ring near bill tip.

Gadwall
Mareca strepera To 21 in. (53 cm)

Blue-winged Teal
Spatula discors To 16 in. (40 cm)

WATERBIRDS

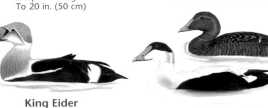
Harlequin Duck
Histrionicus histrionicus To 17 in. (43 cm)

Bufflehead
Bucephala albeola To 15 in. (38 cm)

Common Goldeneye
Bucephala clangula To 20 in. (50 cm)

Barrow's Goldeneye
Bucephala islandica To 20 in. (50 cm)
Male has a white facial crescent.

King Eider
Somateria spectabilis To 2 ft. (60 cm)

Common Eider
Somateria mollissima To 28 in. (70 cm)
Note sloping head profile.

Ruddy Duck
Oxyura jamaicensis To 16 in. (40 cm)
Note cocked tail.

Lesser Scaup
Aythya affinis To 18 in. (45 cm)
Note peaked crown.

Greater Scaup
Aythya marila To 20 in. (50 cm)
Note rounded head.

Surf Scoter
Melanitta perspicillata To 20 in. (50 cm)

Black Scoter
Melanitta americana To 20 in. (50 cm)

White-winged Scoter
Melanitta fusca To 23 in. (58 cm)

WATERBIRDS

Fulvous Whistling-Duck
Dendrocygna bicolor To 20 in. (50 cm)
Tawny duck has a white side stripe.

Muscovy Duck
Cairina moschata To 32 in. (80 cm)
Tropical species was introduced to parks throughout the country. May be black or white. Males have 'warty' faces.

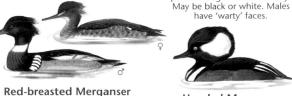
Red-breasted Merganser
Mergus serrator To 27 in. (68 cm)
Note thin bill and prominent head crest.

Hooded Merganser
Lophodytes cucullatus To 20 in. (50 cm)
Note white head crest and thin bill.

Common Merganser
Mergus merganser To 27 in. (68 cm)

Masked Duck
Nomonyx dominicus To 13 in. (33 cm)
Male has a black mask.

NEARSHORE & WADING BIRDS

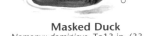
Great Cormorant
Phalacrocorax carbo To 40 in. (1 m)
Note white throat patch.

Double-crested Cormorant
Phalacrocorax auritus To 3 ft. (90 cm)
Note orange-yellow throat patch.

American Coot
Fulica americana To 16 in. (40 cm)

Common Gallinule
Gallinula galeata To 14 in. (35 cm)

Anhinga
Anhinga anhinga To 3 ft. (90 cm)

Purple Gallinule
Porphyrio martinicus To 13 in. (33 cm)

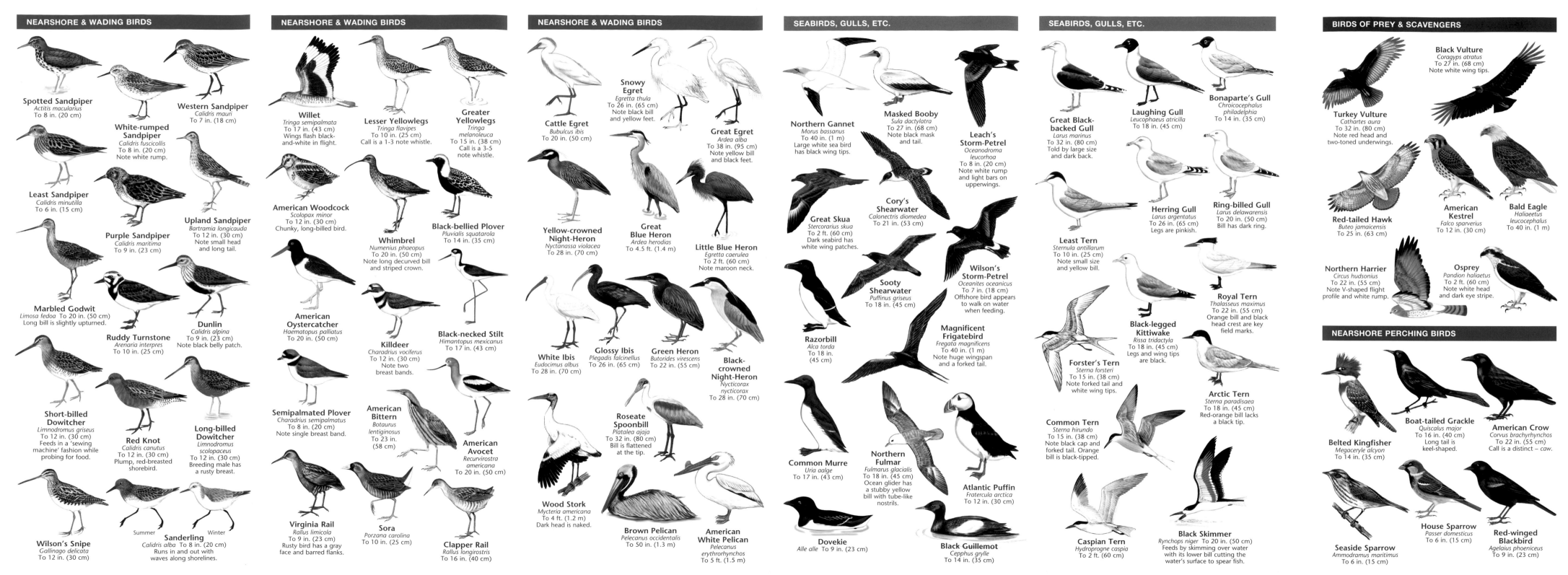

NEARSHORE & WADING BIRDS

Spotted Sandpiper
Actitis macularius
To 8 in. (20 cm)

White-rumped Sandpiper
Calidris fuscicollis
To 8 in. (20 cm)
Note white rump.

Western Sandpiper
Calidris mauri
To 7 in. (18 cm)

Least Sandpiper
Calidris minutilla
To 6 in. (15 cm)

Purple Sandpiper
Calidris maritima
To 9 in. (23 cm)

Upland Sandpiper
Bartramia longicauda
To 12 in. (30 cm)
Note small head
and long tail.

Marbled Godwit
Limosa fedoa To 20 in. (50 cm)
Long bill is slightly upturned.

Ruddy Turnstone
Arenaria interpres
To 10 in. (25 cm)

Dunlin
Calidris alpina
To 9 in. (23 cm)
Note black belly patch.

Short-billed Dowitcher
Limnodromus griseus
To 12 in. (30 cm)
Feeds in a 'sewing
machine' fashion while
probing for food.

Red Knot
Calidris canutus
To 12 in. (30 cm)
Plump, red-breasted
shorebird.

Long-billed Dowitcher
Limnodromus scolopaceus
To 12 in. (30 cm)
Breeding male has
a rusty breast.

Wilson's Snipe
Gallinago delicata
To 12 in. (30 cm)

Sanderling
Calidris alba To 8 in. (20 cm)
Runs in and out with
waves along shorelines.
Summer / Winter

NEARSHORE & WADING BIRDS

Willet
Tringa semipalmata
To 17 in. (43 cm)
Wings flash black-
and-white in flight.

Lesser Yellowlegs
Tringa flavipes
To 10 in. (25 cm)
Call is a 1-3 note whistle.

Greater Yellowlegs
Tringa melanoleuca
To 15 in. (38 cm)
Call is a 3-5
note whistle.

American Woodcock
Scolopax minor
To 12 in. (30 cm)
Chunky, long-billed bird.

Whimbrel
Numenius phaeopus
To 20 in. (50 cm)
Note long decurved bill
and striped crown.

Black-bellied Plover
Pluvialis squatarola
To 14 in. (35 cm)

American Oystercatcher
Haematopus palliatus
To 20 in. (50 cm)

Killdeer
Charadrius vociferus
To 12 in. (30 cm)
Note two
breast bands.

Black-necked Stilt
Himantopus mexicanus
To 17 in. (43 cm)

Semipalmated Plover
Charadrius semipalmatus
To 8 in. (20 cm)
Note single breast band.

American Bittern
Botaurus lentiginosus
To 23 in. (58 cm)

American Avocet
Recurvirostra americana
To 20 in. (50 cm)

Virginia Rail
Rallus limicola
To 9 in. (23 cm)
Rusty bird has a gray
face and barred flanks.

Sora
Porzana carolina
To 10 in. (25 cm)

Clapper Rail
Rallus longirostris
To 16 in. (40 cm)

NEARSHORE & WADING BIRDS

Cattle Egret
Bubulcus ibis
To 20 in. (50 cm)

Snowy Egret
Egretta thula
To 26 in. (65 cm)
Note black bill
and yellow feet.

Great Egret
Ardea alba
To 38 in. (95 cm)
Note yellow bill
and black feet.

Yellow-crowned Night-Heron
Nyctanassa violacea
To 28 in. (70 cm)

Great Blue Heron
Ardea herodias
To 4.5 ft. (1.4 m)

Little Blue Heron
Egretta caerulea
To 2 ft. (60 cm)
Note maroon neck.

White Ibis
Eudocimus albus
To 28 in. (70 cm)

Glossy Ibis
Plegadis falcinellus
To 26 in. (65 cm)

Green Heron
Butorides virescens
To 22 in. (55 cm)

Black-crowned Night-Heron
Nycticorax nycticorax
To 28 in. (70 cm)

Roseate Spoonbill
Platalea ajaja
To 32 in. (80 cm)
Bill is flattened
at the tip.

Wood Stork
Mycteria americana
To 4 ft. (1.2 m)
Dark head is naked.

Brown Pelican
Pelecanus occidentalis
To 50 in. (1.3 m)

American White Pelican
Pelecanus erythrorhynchos
To 5 ft. (1.5 m)

SEABIRDS, GULLS, ETC.

Northern Gannet
Morus bassanus
To 40 in. (1 m)
Large white sea bird
has black wing tips.

Masked Booby
Sula dactylatra
To 27 in. (68 cm)
Note black mask
and tail.

Leach's Storm-Petrel
Oceanodroma leucorhoa
To 8 in. (20 cm)
Note white rump
and light bars on
upperwings.

Great Skua
Stercorarius skua
To 2 ft. (60 cm)
Dark seabird has
white wing patches.

Cory's Shearwater
Calonectris diomedea
To 21 in. (53 cm)

Sooty Shearwater
Puffinus griseus
To 18 in. (45 cm)

Wilson's Storm-Petrel
Oceanites oceanicus
To 7 in. (18 cm)
Offshore bird appears
to walk on water
when feeding.

Razorbill
Alca torda
To 18 in.
(45 cm)

Magnificent Frigatebird
Fregata magnificens
To 40 in. (1 m)
Note huge wingspan
and a forked tail.

Common Murre
Uria aalge
To 17 in. (43 cm)

Northern Fulmar
Fulmarus glacialis
To 18 in. (45 cm)
Ocean glider has
a stubby yellow
bill with tube-like
nostrils.

Atlantic Puffin
Fratercula arctica
To 12 in. (30 cm)

Dovekie
Alle alle To 9 in. (23 cm)

Black Guillemot
Cepphus grylle
To 14 in. (35 cm)

SEABIRDS, GULLS, ETC.

Great Black-backed Gull
Larus marinus
To 32 in. (80 cm)
Told by large size
and dark back.

Laughing Gull
Leucophaeus atricilla
To 18 in. (45 cm)

Bonaparte's Gull
Chroicocephalus philadelphia
To 14 in. (35 cm)

Herring Gull
Larus argentatus
To 26 in. (65 cm)
Legs are pinkish.

Ring-billed Gull
Larus delawarensis
To 20 in. (50 cm)
Bill has dark ring.

Least Tern
Sternula antillarum
To 10 in. (25 cm)
Note small size
and yellow bill.

Royal Tern
Thalasseus maximus
To 22 in. (55 cm)
Orange bill and black
head crest are key
field marks.

Forster's Tern
Sterna forsteri
To 15 in. (38 cm)
Note forked tail and
white wing tips.

Black-legged Kittiwake
Rissa tridactyla
To 18 in. (45 cm)
Legs and wing tips
are black.

Arctic Tern
Sterna paradisaea
To 18 in. (45 cm)
Red-orange bill lacks
a black tip.

Common Tern
Sterna hirundo
To 15 in. (38 cm)
Note black cap and
forked tail. Orange
bill is black-tipped.

Black Skimmer
Rynchops niger To 20 in. (50 cm)
Feeds by skimming over water
with its lower bill cutting the
water's surface to spear fish.

Caspian Tern
Hydroprogne caspia
To 2 ft. (60 cm)

BIRDS OF PREY & SCAVENGERS

Black Vulture
Coragyps atratus
To 27 in. (68 cm)
Note white wing tips.

Turkey Vulture
Cathartes aura
To 32 in. (80 cm)
Note red head and
two-toned underwings.

Red-tailed Hawk
Buteo jamaicensis
To 25 in. (63 cm)

American Kestrel
Falco sparverius
To 12 in. (30 cm)

Bald Eagle
Haliaeetus leucocephalus
To 40 in. (1 m)

Northern Harrier
Circus hudsonius
To 22 in. (55 cm)
Note V-shaped flight
profile and white rump.

Osprey
Pandion haliaetus
To 2 ft. (60 cm)
Note white head
and dark eye stripe.

NEARSHORE PERCHING BIRDS

Belted Kingfisher
Megaceryle alcyon
To 14 in. (35 cm)

Boat-tailed Grackle
Quiscalus major
To 16 in. (40 cm)
Long tail is
keel-shaped.

American Crow
Corvus brachyrhynchos
To 22 in. (55 cm)
Call is a distinct – caw.

Seaside Sparrow
Ammodramus maritimus
To 6 in. (15 cm)

House Sparrow
Passer domesticus
To 6 in. (15 cm)

Red-winged Blackbird
Agelaius phoeniceus
To 9 in. (23 cm)